What Do You Know About
THE SUN?

I LIKE SPACE!

Carmen Bredeson

asteroids (AS tur oydz)
Rocks from space.

comets (KAH mets)
Big balls of dust and ice in space.

core (KORE)
The center part of something.

energy (EH nur jee)
Light and heat.

solar (SOH lur)
Having to do with the Sun.

temperature (TEM pruh chur)
How hot or cold something is.

CONTENTS

What is the solar system?

The solar system is the Sun and its family.
Everything that goes around the Sun is
part of this family. It includes the Earth
and other planets, moons, asteroids,
and comets.

comet

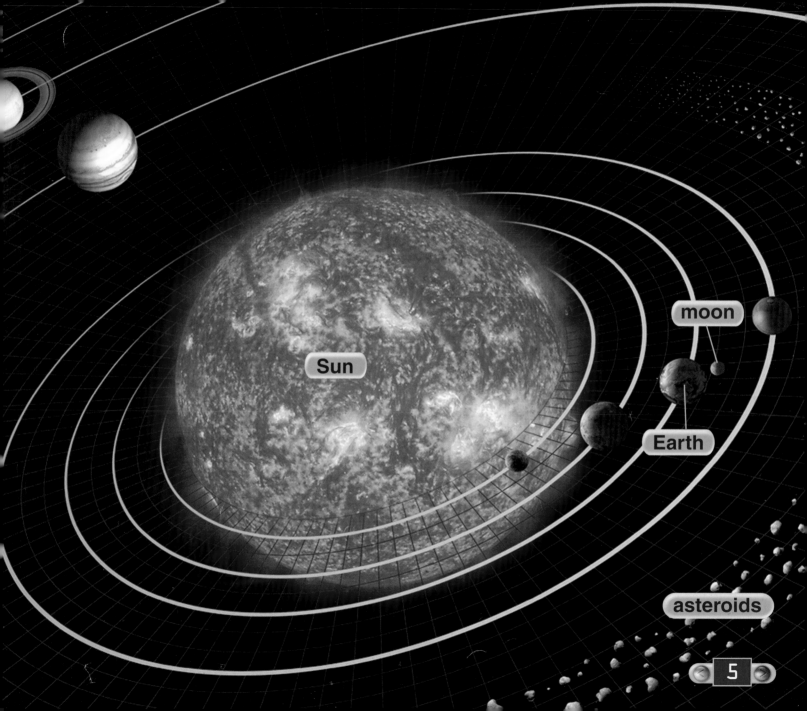

Sun

moon

Earth

asteroids

What is the Sun?

The Sun is a star. From Earth, other stars look like tiny lights. Our Sun looks big because it is much closer to Earth than other stars.

How are stars made?

Stars are made when gas and dust in space form a giant spinning ball. As the gas is pressed tighter and tighter, the ball gets very hot. The gas turns into energy. The energy comes to Earth as heat and light.

Fun Fact

It takes eight minutes for sunlight to reach Earth.

Hundreds of stars are born in this large cloud of gas in space.

How far is the Sun from Earth?

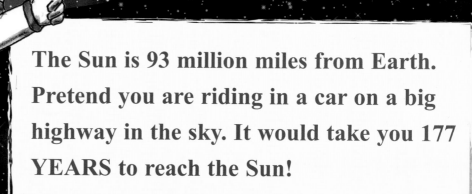

The Sun is 93 million miles from Earth. Pretend you are riding in a car on a big highway in the sky. It would take you 177 YEARS to reach the Sun!

How big is the Sun?

Our Sun is a medium-sized star, but it is MUCH bigger than Earth. More than a million Earths could fit inside the Sun. Medium-sized stars burn their gas more slowly, so they last longer than big stars.

Fun Fact

The hottest part of the Sun is its center, called the core.

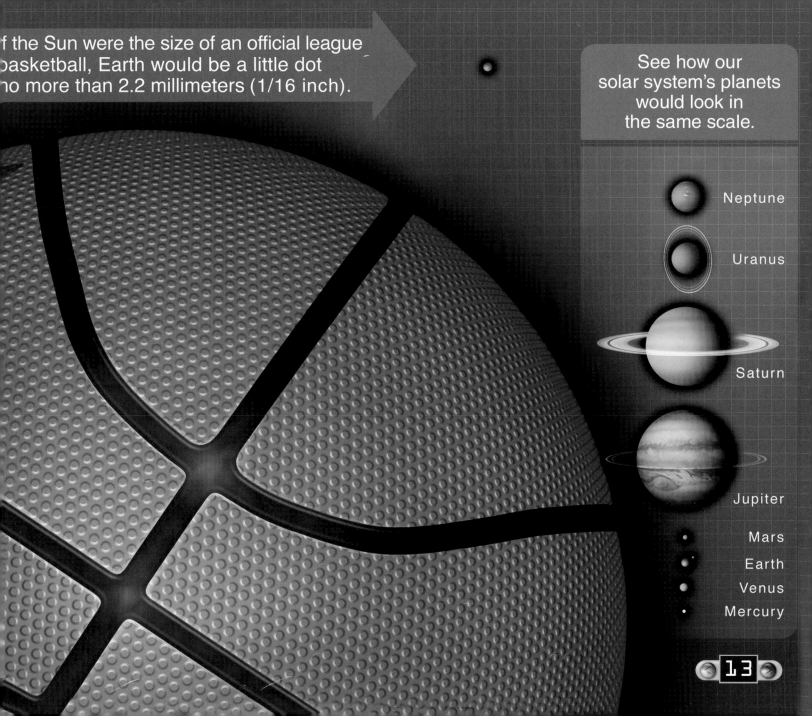

If the Sun were the size of an official league basketball, Earth would be a little dot no more than 2.2 millimeters (1/16 inch).

See how our solar system's planets would look in the same scale.

Neptune

Uranus

Saturn

Jupiter

Mars

Earth

Venus

Mercury

Why is the Sun yellow?

Stars are many different colors.
Very hot stars look blue.
The coolest stars look red.
The Sun is just the right
temperature to look yellow.

red star

blue star

Could you stand on the Sun?

The Sun is made of gas. It does not have hard ground like Earth. You could not stand on the Sun's surface. It would be like trying to stand on a cloud. Plus, it is way too hot!

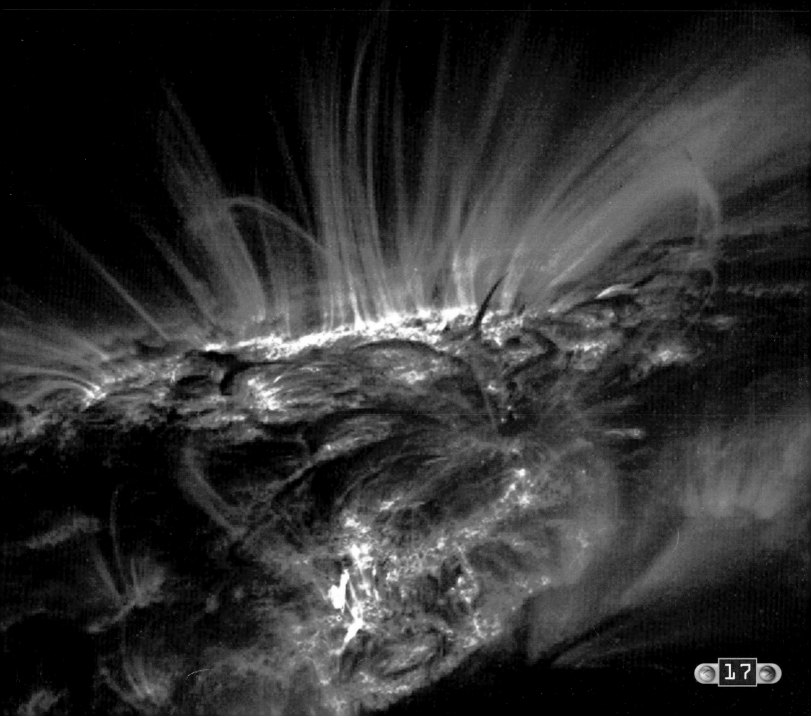

Why does Earth need the Sun?

The Sun keeps Earth warm.

Without the Sun, plants would not grow.

People and animals would freeze.

The Sun gives us the light, heat, and food that we need to live.

19

Fun Fact

Plants on Earth turn
sunlight into food.

What is solar power?

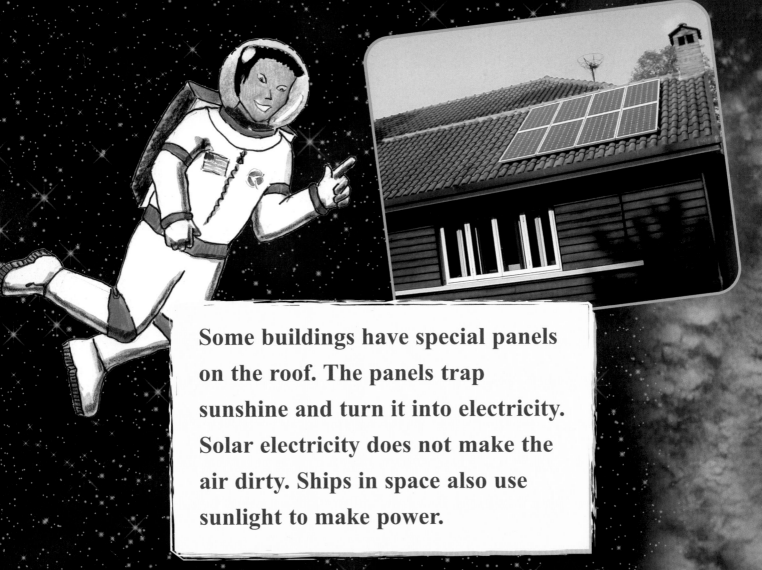

Some buildings have special panels on the roof. The panels trap sunshine and turn it into electricity. Solar electricity does not make the air dirty. Ships in space also use sunlight to make power.

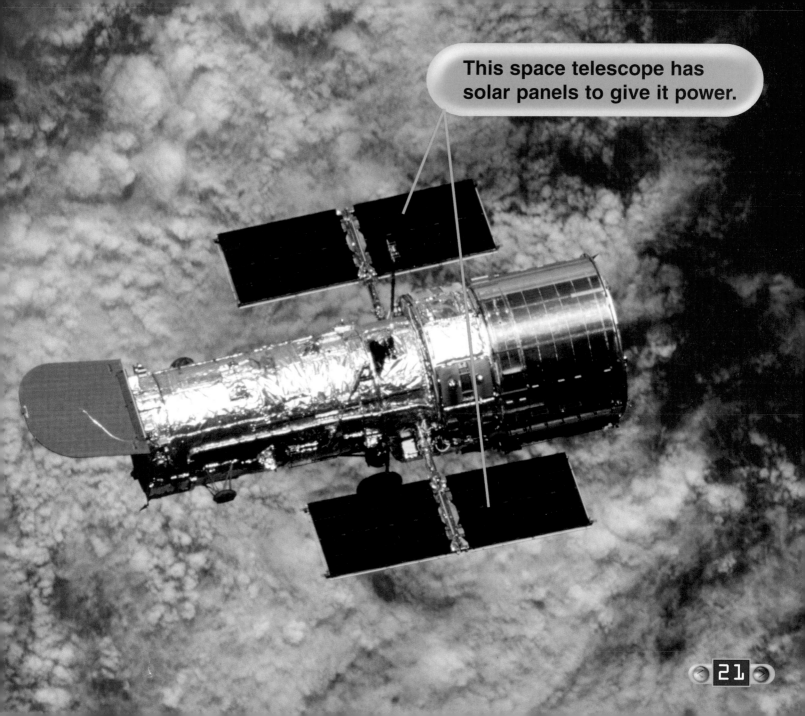

This space telescope has solar panels to give it power.

How can sunlight be unsafe?

People and plants need sunlight to live. But too much sunlight can burn your skin and hurt your eyes. Sunscreen, clothing, and sunglasses help protect people from too much Sun.

Can you look at the Sun?

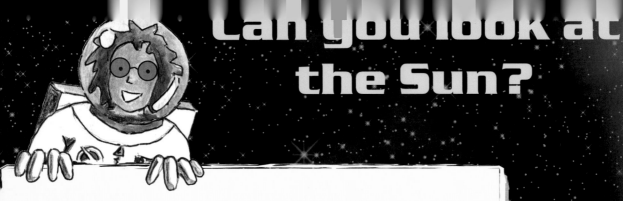

No! Looking at the Sun could make you blind. The Sun is too bright for your eyes, even when you are wearing sunglasses. Scientists use special machines to look at the Sun.

Fun Fact

Sundials were the first clocks. They use a shadow from the Sun's light to tell the time of day. Sundials do not work at night.

Scientists use this large telescope to look at the Sun.

How long will the Sun shine?

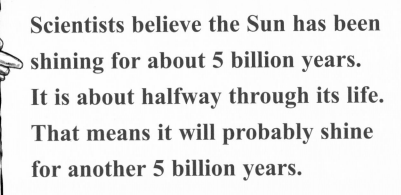

Scientists believe the Sun has been shining for about 5 billion years. It is about halfway through its life. That means it will probably shine for another 5 billion years.

Where does the Sun go at night?

The Sun does not go anywhere.

It is Earth that moves.

Earth turns all the way around each day.

It is day on the side of Earth facing the Sun.

It is night on the side of Earth facing away from the Sun.

Sun

It is day on this
side of Earth.

It is night on this
side of Earth.

Earth

Who studies the Sun?

Astronomers use special telescopes to study the Sun.

Aerospace engineers make space ships that fly around the Sun.

Solar engineers design buildings that use energy from the Sun.

Computer scientists keep track of temperatures on the Sun.

LEARN MORE

Books

Bredeson, Carmen. *The Solar System*. New York: Children's
    Press, 2003.

Stott, Carole. *Stars and Planets*. New York: Kingfisher, 2005.

Winrich, Ralph. *The Sun*. Mankato, Minnesota: Capstone
    Press, 2005.

Web Sites

High Altitude Observatory

<http://www.hao.ucar.edu/Public/education/basic.html>

Astronomy for Kids

<http://www.kidsastronomy.com>

INDEX

To Kate, our shining star

Enslow Elementary, an imprint of Enslow Publishers, Inc.
Enslow Elementary® is a registered trademark of Enslow Publishers, Inc.

Copyright © 2008 by Enslow Publishers, Inc.

Library of Congress Cataloging-in-Publication Data

Bredeson, Carmen.
    What do you know about the sun? / Carmen Bredeson.
        p. cm. — (I like space!)
    Summary: "Introduces early readers to subjects about space in Q&A format"—
Provided by publisher.
    Includes bibliographical references and index.
    ISBN-13: 978-0-7660-2941-5
    ISBN-10: 0-7660-2941-7
    1. Sun—Juvenile literature. I. Title.
    QB521.5.B745 2008
    523.7—dc22   2007002746

Printed in the United States of America

10 9 8 7 6 5 4 3 2 1

To Our Readers: We have done our best to make sure all Internet Addresses in this book were
active and appropriate when we went to press. However, the author and the publisher have
no control over and assume no liability for the material available on those Internet sites or on
other Web sites they may link to. Any comments or suggestions can be sent by e-mail to
comments@enslow.com or to the address on the back cover.

Illustration Credits: Carl M. Feryok

Photo Credits: Akira Fujii/ESA, p. 15; Courtesy NASA/JPL—Caltech, pp. 2, 4–5; Enslow
Publishers, Inc., p. 29; Gerald & Buff Corsi/Visuals Unlimited, pp. 24–25; Gerard
Lodriguss/Photo Researchers, Inc., p. 6; © istockphoto.com/Roberta Casaliggi, p. 20; © 2007
Jupiterimages Corporation, pp. 18–19, 22–23 (boy), 26–27; NASA, pp. 1, 2, 10, 11, 21; NASA
and European Space Agency, p. 13; NASA and the Hubble Heritage Team, p. 9; Shutterstock,
blue starfield background and pp. 7, 14, 22–23 (beach), 23 (girls); TRACE Project, NASA,
p. 17.

Cover Photo: NASA

Series Literacy Consultant:
Allan A. De Fina, Ph.D.
Past President of the New Jersey Reading Association
Chairperson, Department of Literacy Education
New Jersey City University, Jersey City, New Jersey

Series Science Consultant:
Marianne J. Dyson
Former NASA Flight Controller
Science writer
www.mdyson.com

Enslow Elementary
an imprint of
Enslow Publishers, Inc.
40 Industrial Road
Box 398
Berkeley Heights, NJ 07922
USA

http://www.enslow.com